Cryptography
By Solis Tech

Cryptography Theory & Practice Made Easy!

2nd Edition

Cryptography (2nd Edition): Cryptography Theory & Practice Made Easy!

Table of Contents

Introduction

I want to thank you and congratulate you for downloading the book, *Cryptography*.

Cryptography has always been fascinating not just because of its enigmatic nature but also because and it has been used for various applications. One of the most captivating uses of cryptography is in the law enforcement and the military. It has been used by many military men to communicate information secretly.

In January 6, 1995, there was an apartment fire in Manila, Philippines. When the police responded to the fire, they saw a laptop and some chemicals and bomb-making materials. An open file found in the laptop revealed that there is a plot to simultaneously bomb twelve US airlines. The potential death toll is about four thousand people. These files utilized encryption software that contains various codes. The information technology department of the Philippine police decoded some of the files using a special computer program and found attack plots and bomb-making recipes.

The evidence that was uncovered during the operation pointed to one of the most notorious terrorists at that time – Ramzi Ahmed Yousef. He was wanted for his involvement in the first World Trade Center Bombing in 1993. After decrypting the message, the Philippine police uncovered Yousef's plots and within six weeks, he was arrested and under the custody of the Federal Bureau of Investigation or FBI.

This was considered a big victory for the international law enforcement. The decryption of the bombing plot and Yousef's arrest revealed the importance of cryptology – the science and art of making and breaking codes.

For centuries, codes and cryptology have been used and controlled by the governments and military agencies. It is used in diplomacy, warfare, and espionage. But, with modern technology, the use of codes by individuals has exploded. This heightened the needs for codes. Nowadays, codes are used to keep the information private on the internet. It is used at ATMs and in several businesses.

Cryptography (2nd Edition): Cryptography Theory & Practice Made Easy!

The need for data security is constantly increasing. It is no surprise that there is also an increased need for strong security measures. Cryptography keeps your systems and information safe from unscrupulous individual.

This book contains tips and techniques on how to build cryptosystems – even if you're just a complete beginner.

This eBook will help you learn about the history and basic principles of cryptography. It will teach you the different aspects of message encryption. In addition, you will learn how to establish cryptosystems. Aside from discussing modern/digital encryption schemes, this book will teach you how to use different types of "practical" ciphers.

Thanks again for downloading this book. I hope you enjoy it!

Chapter 1: Cryptography – History and Basic Concepts

The Origin of Cryptography

During the ancient times, people needed to do two things: (1) to share information and (2) protect the information they are sharing. These things forced individuals to "encode" their messages. This "encoding" process protects the message in a way that only the intended recipient can understand the information. That means the data will remain secure even if unauthorized parties get access to it.

The art and science of protecting information is now known as "cryptography." The term "cryptography" was formed by fusing two Greek terms, "Krypto" (which means "hidden") and "graphene" (which means writing).

According to historians, cryptography and "normal" writing were born at the same time. As human civilizations progressed, people organized themselves into groups, clans, and kingdoms. These organizations led to the creation of concepts such as wars, powers, sovereignty, and politics. Obviously, these ideas involve information that cannot be shared with ordinary citizens. The group leaders needed to send and receive information through protected means. Thus, cryptography continued to evolve.

The earliest known code was an encryption carved into the rock by an Egyptian scribe in 1900 BC. Another early code was used for secrecy. The tiny an enciphered tablet found on the banks of the Tigress River that was created in 1500 BC contained a hidden formula for an ancient secret art - pottery. The ancient Greeks also created their own coding methods.

The Contributions of Egyptians and Romans

1. Egyptians

The oldest sample of cryptography can be found in Egypt. Ancient Egyptians used hieroglyphs (i.e. a system of writing that involves symbols and images) to share and record pieces of information. In general, these symbols and images are only intelligible to the priests who transmitted messages on behalf of the pharaohs. Here is a sample hieroglyph:

Fig. 1 - Egyptian Hieroglyphs

Several thousands of years later (around 600 to 500 BC), Egyptian scholars started to use simple substitution codes. This style of encoding involved the replacement and/or combination of two or more alphabets using a secret rule. This rule was considered as the "key" in retrieving the real message from the coded "garbage."

2. Romans

Ancient Romans used a system of cryptography known as the Caesar (or Shift) Cipher. This system depends on moving each letter of the message by a certain number (three is the most popular choice). To decode the information, the recipient simply needs to "move" the letters back using the same number. Here is an example:

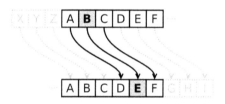

Fig. 2 – Caesar Cipher

The Persians also have their own coding methods. One of the subordinates of a Persian king wanted to revolt against his master. He has an agent inside the palace. This agent sent a message to this man saying that their men are already ready for revolution. The agent shaved the head of his slave and tattooed the word "revolt" on his head. He waited for his slave's hair to grow to conceal the message. Then, he sent the slave to the subordinate's palace. Once the man got the slave, he shaved the head and he saw the word "revolt". He knew that his men were already ready for the revolution and they successfully revolted against the King.

A new instrument was used in Sparta to encrypt messages. This tool is called the **Scytale**. The Spartans wrap a cloth around the stick, then they would write the message on the side. You can read the message when wrapped around the stick but when you unwrap it, the message was scrambled. This way, the message is concealed. The message was sent from one military officer to another unwrapped.

Photo Source: oxfordmathcenter.com

Every code has a key, a secret method of scrambling messages used by the sender and the receiver. Julius Ceasar enciphered his communication method by enciphering different letters by moving the letters three spaces from the right. But, with the collapse of the Roman Empire in 500 AD, the Roman and European cryptology entered into a dark age. Encryption declined in Europe during this time.

But, another civilization was rising in the east by 900 AD, the Arab culture became one of the most literate cultures in the world. The study of codes became more and more popular in the East during this time. The Arabs were the first to record the methods of re-positioning the letters and swapping them with other words. They also used substitution wherein they replaced the letters with numbers and symbols. The Arabs also first established a system of code-breaking that employs mathematical, symbols, and frequency analysis. They decipher codes by analyzing the frequency of the appearance of the letters in the text. The letter with the most frequency is most likely the key.

In 1466, an Italian architect named Leon Battista Alberti discovered the greatest cryptographic invention during this time. It is called the **Alberti cipher disk**. It is a system of rotating cipher disk with two strings of letters. By scrambling and mixing the letters randomly, this method was the first to challenge the Arab code breaking method of frequency analysis. Previous systems just replaced A with D only one at the time. The cipher disk used a disk in which these letter combinations could be changed from time to time. So, as a consequence, A would be replaced not only by one letter but by many other letters. This was called poly-alphabetic mini alphabet substitution and it was the basis for many modern cipher systems.

A French diplomat improved this cipher system in 1586 by creating a grid of twenty six cipher alphabets. Each system was coded one letter ahead from the last. In coding and de-coding communications using visionary square, this could be calculated on a piece of paper so you don't have to carry around a disk.

Unfortunately, Mary, Queen of Scots, was not aware of this new cryptographic development. In 1568, Mary was locked away by her cousin and rival, Queen Elizabeth I of England. In 1586, a group of Catholics planned to rescue Mary. They plan to place her on the English throne after completing their plot to kill Queen Elizabeth. The plot was communicated through secret coded letters. However, the greatest mistake of Queen Mary's camp was that they thought that their cipher system was secure. They thought that it cannot be deciphered by Queen Elizabeth's code breakers. Alas, the English code breakers were able to decode the communications and the plot was discovered. Queen Elizabeth then decided to execute Queen Mary. This incident is a testament that the proficiency in cryptology is essential in successfully trampling a regime.

By the 1700s, each European country owned a black chamber. This black chamber was used for deciphering cryptic messages and codes. They employ the best and the brightest mathematicians across Europe.

The discovery of the telegraph made it possible to send a message quickly from city to city and country to country. In fact, a lot of historians would agree that the telegraph made the United States a very powerful country. The discovery of the telegraph also raised the necessity of cryptology.

In 1844, Samuel Morris invented the Morse Code -- a series of electrical dots and dashes to communicate over the telephone. The code was public, so it's quite easy to intercept and decipher the codes. Then, the radio was invented by a great Italian physicist named Guglielmo Marconi. The radio was used as the new method of communication during this time. However, the radio is not secure and it is easily intercepted. As a result, military men decided to encrypt the messages by sending it in morse codes.

The greatest and most important code-breaking event in the entire history of cryptology happened on January 17, 1917. The British military intercepted a telegram from Berlin containing the highest diplomatic code in Germany – 0075. This is a mind-numbing code system that contains thousands of code groups. The secret message was from Arthur Zimmerman, the foreign minister of Germany at that time. The recipient of the message is the German ambassador in Washington who is also the ambassador to Mexico. The message is supposed to be deciphered in Washington and then sent to Venustiano Carranza, the Mexican President at that time. The message was encrypted on the American undersea telegraph cable. Then it was transmitted from Berlin to Washington.

The British intelligence group intercepted the message in Washington and they immediately suspect that it is important. The British has already broken the old German code, but this one contains the new 0075 code. So, the British intelligence officers were not able to decipher the message. But, the staff of the ambassador made a grave mistake. After they deciphered the message, they re-encrypted it using the old German code book and sent it to the office of the Mexican president through the telegraph. The British cryptanalysts have already broken the old German code. So, they sat down and began to decipher the codes and the message in chunks. They figured out the patterns using paper and pencil. The process was painstaking but it was worth it.

Within days, the British cryptanalysts hacked and deciphered the message. They discovered the true meaning of Zimmerman's secret message. The message outlined the intent of Germany to initiate a full-force submarine warfare to suppress Britain. They plan to carry out the plan on Febuary 1, 1917. America and Britain are great allies. So, to keep America at bay, the German ambassador proposed that Mexico should initiate a war against America and reclaim Texas, Mexico City, and Arizona. Zimmerman also asked Carranza to persuade Japan to attack the United States. Zimmerman assured the Mexican president that Germany will finance the attacks.

The British cryptanalysts were desperate to transmit the message to the United States without alerting Germany that the message has been intercepted and deciphered. So, they approached the Americans secretly and revealed the true meaning of the telegram. After six weeks, America declared a war against Germany.

During the World War I, a German electrical engineer named Arthur Servius independently created electrical encryption machines. These machines revolutionized cryptography by mechanizing the production of codes with millions of potential variations. This machine has twenty six electrical contacts on one side and twenty six electrical contacts on the other side wired at random. So when you type A, it will go through the electrical contacts and it types another letter. This machine has several cipher wheels. In 1920s, Arthur Servius mass produced his cryptology machine called Enigma. The machine was used by the German military in 1920s to 1940s.

Poland, who's caught between German and Russia, was desperate for intelligence. The Polish set up a major crypto-analyst bureau and hired a group of brilliant mathematicians including Marian Rejewski. Rejewski reconstructed the wiring of the Enigma machine without even seeing one. He built his own model of the German military encryption machine Enigma. At the time, only a few hundreds of units of the German Enigma existed and all of these machines are kept under tight control of the German Army. Then, in 1931, a German traitor supplied background information on how to use the Enigma machine. This information acted as a supplement to Rejewski's guesswork.

However, the Germans routinely change the daily key. The daily key was distributed in a monthly code book that guides both the sender and receiver in sending messages. To find the daily key, Rejewski built and completed the replicas of six Enigma machines together. They ran through more than a thousand indicator settings. He called his new machine "Bomba" because of its ticking noise. It was a machine created to intercept another machine.

Alan Turing, a mathematical genius, was recruited by the British army to decode the German Enigma machine. Turing created his own machine called "Bombe". It has 180 routers that are grounded letter by letter. Round 20 letters are grounded every second until the routers hit the correct one. By this time, the British military employs hundreds of codebreakers working in shifts to decipher hundred of messages that are encrypted by the German Enigma code machines. These British coders lived and worked in Bletchley Park.

In 1943, a British engineer named Tommy Flowers created Colossus. A machine that moved code-breaking from electro-mechanical to purely electronic. This worked much faster. This machine was able to break Germany's most complex coding system – the 12 router Lawrence machine which was used by Germany's top commanders including Adolf Hitler.

Colossus was a computer that's capable of reading paper tape and five thousand characters every second. This machine played a major role in the victory of the battle of the Atlanta and the war in North Africa.

Code breaking shortened the war and saved millions of lives. It also highlighted the power of brains over bullets. It also launched the computer age.

In another part of the Pacific, the Americans were launching their own codes. They hired a number of bilingual Navajo speakers who act as the standard communication officers in the Pacific. The Navajo code is a top secret. In fact, the Navajo speakers were not allowed to talk openly about their role during the Pacific war. The involvement of the speakers was only made public in 1968. They were finally honored in 1982 for their exceptional contribution during the Pacific war. What's fascinating is that the Navajo code was not broken even up to this day.

But the task of breaking complicated codes continues even up to this modern age of computers. For centuries, the governments and military groups controlled cryptology. But, times are changing. After the World War II, inventors designed machines that would produce code that have infinite complexity. Code breakers now have to work 25 times more just to break codes.

In 1952, US President Harry Truman founded the NSA or the National Security Agency. The National Security Agency has the pool of the best computer and cryptology experts in the United states. The agency is in charge of intercepting and decrypting intelligence messages from all over the world. By the 1970s, more businesses use computers to encrypt information and it is used not only in the military but also in various businesses and organizations.

Cryptography – Fundamental Concepts

Encryption – This is the process of converting information into an unintelligible form. It helps in securing the privacy of the message while it is being sent to the recipient.

Decryption – This process is the exact opposite of encryption. Here, the encoded message is returned to its natural form.

Important Note: Encryption and decryption require specific rules in converting the data involved. These rules are known as the key. Sometimes, a single key is used to encrypt and decrypt information. However, there are certain scenarios where these two processes require different sets of keys.

Plaintext and Ciphertext – The term plaintext refers to data that can be read and used without the application of special techniques. Ciphertext, on the other hand, refers to data that cannot be read easily: the recipient needs to use certain decryption processes to get the "real" message.

Authentication – This is probably one of the most important aspects of cryptography. Basically, authentication serves as a proof that the information was sent by the party claimed in the encoded message.

Let's illustrate this concept using a simple example: John sent a message to Jane. However, before replying, Jane wants to make sure that the message really came from John. This verification procedure can be conducted easily if John does "something" on the message that Jane knows only John can do (e.g. writing his signature, including a secret phrase, folding the letter in a certain way, etc.). Obviously, successful decryption of the message will be useless if the information came from an unwanted source.

Integrity – Loss of integrity is one of the biggest problems faced by people who use cryptography. Basically, loss of integrity occurs whenever the message gets altered while it is being sent to the receiver. Unnecessary and/or unwanted modifications in a message may cause misunderstanding and other issues. Because of this, the message must be protected while it is being delivered. Modern cryptographers accomplish this through the use of a cryptographic hash (i.e. a hash function that is extremely difficult to invert, modify, or recreate).

Non-Repudiation – This concept focuses on ensuring that the sender cannot deny that he/she sent the encoded message. In the example given above, it is important to make sure that John cannot deny the fact that he was the one who sent the message. Modern cryptography prevents this "sender repudiation" using digital signatures.

Remember that the science and the art of cryptography work both ways. It can be used to secure sensitive data and, at the same time, it can be used to break and decipher secure messages.

Chapter 2: The Modern Cryptography

For some people, modern cryptography is the foundation of technology and communications security. This type of cryptography is based on mathematical concepts like the number theory, the probability theory, and the computational-complexity theory. To help you understand modern cryptography, here is a comparison of the "classical" and "modern" types of cryptography.

Classical Cryptography

1. It utilizes common characters (e.g. letters and numbers) directly.

2. It relies heavily on the "obscure is secure" principle. The encryption and decryption processes were considered as confidential information. Only the people involved in the communication can access such data.

3. It needs an entire cryptosystem (will be explained in the next chapter) to complete the "confidential" transfer of information.

Modern Cryptography

1. It relies on modern technology like binary data sequences.

2. The information is encoded through the use of mathematical algorithms accessible to the public. Here, security is achieved through a "secret key" which is used as the foundation for the algorithms. Two factors ensure that "outsiders" cannot access the information even if they have the correct algorithm:

    a. It is extremely difficult to compute such algorithms. Thus, it is hard to extract any information from them.

    b. The absence or presence of secret keys.

3. The encryption doesn't involve the entire cryptosystem. Only the interested parties are required to participate in encoding and decoding the message.

Although many mathematicians still manually compute for keys and use specific formulas for encryption, there are a number of devices that are used for encryption and decryption. Here are some of those devices:

- Motorola STU-II/B
- Motorola STU- III
- Motorola MX300
- Motorola D1118
- Motorola MDT -9100
- AIM
- Fialka
- Teltron GmbH
- Philips PX1000
- AT&T TSD 3600
- UP2101
- PX2000
- Siemens Miniflex
- Siemens M190 Mixer Machine
- AT&T 1100 STU-III
- AT&T 4100 Secure Phone
- AT&T GC 524
- MX 18290
- R-353
- Osobnjak
- Mason
- FSH 3
- HE-100
- Hallicrafters SX-28

- EP1140E

- EP830E

- KVL-3000

Encryption devices are classified into several generations:

1. Electro-mechanical Generation

These products were developed shortly after the World War II. The daily keys for these cryptographic machines are distributed using a paper key list.

2. Vacuum Tubes

These encryption machines were developed in the 1960s and 1970s. Keys for these machines are distributed through punch cards.

3. Integrated Circuits

These machines were developed during the 1980s. This was based on transistor logic and these machines use integrated circuits. The keys were generated through a connector located on the front panel of each integrated circuit device.

4. Electronic Key Distribution

This was used in 1990s. There are a number of electronic key distribution devices that were used by the NSA, including the Motorola Sectel 2500 (STU III).

5. Network Centric Systems

Devices that use network centric systems such as KG-84 were used from year 2000 onwards.

There are tens to hundreds of other cryptographic devices that were used over the years. Cryptography is constantly changing, getting better and better over time.

Chapter 3: Cryptosystem – The Basics

A cryptosystem is the application of cryptographic methods and their appropriate coding environment (also called "infrastructure"). This system is used to add security to technology and communications services. Some people refer to cryptosystems as "cipher systems."

To illustrate the concept of cryptosystems, let's consider the following example:

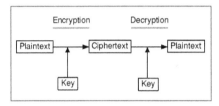

Fig. 3 – A Cryptosystem

In this example, the sender encrypts his message (i.e. the plaintext) through the use of a key. This process converts the plaintext into ciphertext. Once the receiver gets the ciphertext, he uses the same key to decrypt the information. Thus, the ciphertext will be turned into plaintext again.

As you can see, only the parties who have the "key" can access the shared information. Cryptosystems can be divided into these basic components:

- Plaintext – The information that needs to be shared and protected.

- Encryption Algorithm – The mathematical process that uses a plaintext and an encryption key to produce a ciphertext.

- Ciphertext – The coded version of the information. In general, cryptography protects the message itself, not the transmission. That means the coded message is sent through public channels such as emails. Thus, anyone who can access the selected delivery channel can intercept or compromise the message.

- Decryption Algorithm – It is a mathematical process that creates plaintext from any given set of ciphertext and decryption key. Basically, it reverses the encryption process done earlier in the transmission of the message.

- Encryption Key – The value provided by the sender. In creating the ciphertext, the sender enters this key (along with the plaintext) into the encryption algorithm.

- Decryption Key – The value known by the recipient. The decryption key is always related to the encryption key used for the message. However, these keys don't have to be identical. The recipient enters the decryption key and the ciphertext into the decryption algorithm in order to get the plaintext. The collection of all decryption keys for a cryptosystem is known as a "key space."

There are times when an interceptor (also called "attacker") tries to get the encoded message. In general, interceptors are unauthorized entities who want to access the ciphertext and determine the information it contains.

The Two Kinds of Cryptosystems

Currently, cryptosystems are divided into two kinds: (1) Symmetric Key Encryption and (2) Asymmetric Key Encryption. This way of classifying cryptosystems is based on the method of encryption/decryption used for the entire system.

The major difference between the symmetric and asymmetric encryptions is the connection between the encryption and decryption keys. Generally speaking, all cryptosystems involve keys that are closely related. It is impossible to create a decryption key that is totally unrelated to the code's encryption key. Let's discuss each kind of cryptosystems in more detail:

Symmetric Key Encryption

Cryptosystems that belong to this kind have a single key. This key is used to encrypt and decrypt the information being sent. The study of symmetric encryption and systems is known as "symmetric cryptography." Some people refer to symmetric cryptosystems as "secret key" systems. The most popular methods of symmetric key encryption are: IDEA, BLOWFISH, DES (Digital Encryption Standard), and 3DES (Triple-DES).

During the 1960s, 100% of the cryptosystems utilized symmetric encryption. This method of encrypting and decrypting information is so reliable and efficient that it is still being used even today. Businesses that specialize on Communications and Information Technology consider symmetric encryption as the best option available. Since this kind of encryption has distinct advantages over the asymmetric one, it will still be used in the future.

Here are the main characteristics of symmetrically encrypted cryptosystems:

- Before transmitting the message, the sender and the receiver must determine the key that will be used.

- The key must be changed regularly to avoid any intrusion into the cryptosystem.

- A stable form of data transmission must be established to facilitate easy sharing of the key between the involved parties. Since the keys must be changed on a regular basis, this mechanism may prove to be expensive and complicated.

- In an organization composed of "x" individuals, to facilitate two-way communication between any two members, the required number of keys for the entire system is derived using the formula: "$x * (x-1)/2$."

- The keys used are often small (i.e. measured through the number of bits involved), so the encryption and decryption processes are faster and simpler compared to those used for asymmetric systems.

- These cryptosystems do not require high processing capabilities from computer systems. Since the keys used are small and simple, ordinary computers can be used to establish and manage the cryptosystem.

Here are the two problems usually encountered when using this kind of cryptosystem:

- Key Determination – Before any message can be transmitted, the sender and the receiver must determine a specific symmetric key. That means a secure and consistent way of creating keys must be established.

- Trust Issues – Because all the people involved use the same key, symmetric key cryptography requires the sender to trust the receiver, and vice versa. For instance, if one of them shares the key with an unauthorized party, the security of the entire cryptosystem will be ruined.

Modern day communicators say that these two concerns are extremely challenging. Nowadays, people are required to exchange valuable data with non-trusted and non-familiar parties (e.g. seller and buyer relationships). Because of these problems, cryptographers had to develop a new encryption scheme: the asymmetric key encryption.

Types of Symmetric Encryption Algorithms

There are many types of symmetric encryption algorithms, including:

1. Rivest Cipher or RC4

This encryption algorithm was designed by Ron Rivest in 1987. It is a type of stream cipher. It is known for its simplicity and speed. But, experts discovered later one that RC4 has multiple vulnerabilities and it is insecure to some extent.

RC4 normally uses 64 bit and 128 bit key sizes. This algorithm is strong cryptographically and relatively easy to implement. The RC4 or Rivest Cipher has two parts – Pseudo-Random Generation Algorithm and Key Scheduling Algorithm or KSA. The most popular implementation of this algorithm is in SSL and in WEP for 802.11 wireless networks.

Here's a diagram of how RC4 works:

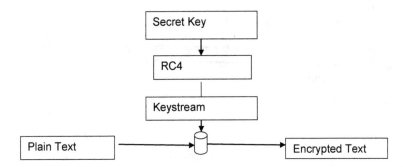

The secret key is the password that's used to encrypt and decrypt the message. The RC4 block in the diagram is nothing but the encryption engine. So what happens is that the user inputs a plain text file with the secret key. Then, the encryption engine generates a key stream and converts the plain text bit by bit into an encrypted text.

RC4 initiates an array of 256 bytes and runs the KSA or key scheduling algorithm on them. The output of the KSA is then plugged into the Pseudo-Random Generation Algorithm which will generate the keystream. Then, the keystream will perform the XOR operation on the data and turn it into encrypted text.

2. RC2

RC2 is also known as ARC2. This was also designed by Ron Rivest. RC stands for Rivest Cipher. The development of this algorithm was supported by Lotus.

It is a 64 bit block cipher that has a variable size key. It uses 18 rounds. The 18 rounds are performed using this interleaved sequence:

- Five mixing rounds

- One mashing round

- Six mixing rounds

- One mashing round

- Five mixing rounds

RC2 uses the key expansion algorithm.

3. RC6

RC6 was also designed by Ron Rivest. The algorithm is patented by RSA Security. It has a block size of 128 bits and it supports key sizes 192, 128, and 256 bits. Leaked reports show that the NSA systems that are used to intercept internet communications produce RC6 UDP or User Diagram Protocol traffic.

4. Serpent

Serpent is a symmetric key algorithm that was designed Lars Knusen, Eli Biham, and Ross Anderson. It has a block size of 128 bits and supports a key size 256, 192, and 128. Serpent has a conservative approach to security as it has a large security margin.

The Serpent cipher is not patented and it is in a public domain. Anyone is free to incorporate this algorithm in their hardware or software implementation.

A number of studies show that the XSL attack can weaken Serpent.

5. Twofish

Twofish is a symmetric block cipher published in 1998 by Counterplane Labs. It has a 128-bit block size. The key size ranges from 128 to 256 bits. It is also optimized for 32-bit CPUs. Two-fish is license-free and unpatented so anyone can use it. Twofish was designed to meet the design criteria of NIST (National Institute of Standards and Technology). It has no weak keys. It is also efficient both on the Intel Pentium and other hardware and software platform. It has a flexible design so it accepts additional key lengths. The design of this algorithm is simple and easy to implement.

6. DES

DES stands for Data Encryption Standard. This was once the most commonly used symmetric-key algorithm for encrypting electronic data. This was developed at IBM in the 1970s. This was used by the NSA in the 70s so many suspected that there is a backdoor to this cipher. Before the rounds, the block is classified into two 32-bit halves. The halves are processed alternately. This process is known as the Feistel scheme.

DES is now considered as unsecured primarily because of its 56-bit key size which is too small.

7. Triple DES

Triple DES or triple data encryption standard. Triple DES uses a key bundle that comprises three DES keys – K1, K2, and K3.

The encryption algorithm of triple DES is:

$$\text{ciphertext} = E_{K_3} (D_{K_2}(E_{K_1}(\text{plaintext})))$$

The decryption algorithms is:

$$\text{plaintext} = D_{K_1} (E_{K_2}(D_{K_3}(\text{ciphertext})))$$

If you noticed, the decryption is the same as encryption.

8. CAST5

CAST5 or CAST128 is a symmetric-key block that's used by many products. In fact, it is the default algorithm of PGP (Pretty Good Privacy) and GPG (GNU Privacy Guard).

Asymmetric Key Encryption

These cryptosystems use different keys for encrypting and decrypting the message. Although the keys involved are dissimilar, they still have a logical and/or mathematical relationship. It is impossible to extract the message using a decryption key that is totally unrelated to the encryption key.

According to cryptographers, this mode of encryption was developed during the 20th century. It was developed in order to overcome the challenges related to symmetric key cryptosystems. The main characteristics of this encryption scheme are:

- Each member of the cryptosystem should have two different keys – a public key and a private key. When one of these keys is used for encryption, the other one must be used for decryption.

- The private key is considered as confidential information. Each member must protect the private key at all times. The public key, on the other hand, can be shared with anyone. Thus, public keys can be placed in a public repository. As such, some people refer to this scheme as "public key encryption."

- Although the private and public keys are mathematically related, it is practically impossible to determine a key using its "partner."

- When Member1 wants to send information to Member2, he needs to do three things:

    o Obtain Member2's public key from the public repository.

    o Encrypt the message.

    o Transmit the message to Member2. Member2 will acquire the original message using his private key.

- This mode of encryption involves larger and longer keys. That means its encryption and decryption processes are slower compared to those of symmetric encryption.

- The asymmetric key encryption requires high processing power from the computers used in the cryptosystem.

Symmetric key encryption is easy to comprehend. The asymmetric one, however, is quite difficult to understand.

You may be wondering as to how the encryption and decryption keys become related and yet prevent intruders from acquiring a key using its "partner." The answer to this question lies in mathematical principles. Today, cryptographers can create encryption keys based on these principles. Actually, the concept of asymmetric key cryptography is new: system intruders are not yet familiar with how this encryption works.

Here is the main problem associated with asymmetric key cryptosystems:

- Each member needs to trust the cryptosystem. He/she has to believe that the public key used for the transmission is the correct one. That person must convince himself that the keys in the public repository are safe from system intruders.

To secure the cryptosystem, companies often use a PKI (Public Key Infrastructure) that involves a reputable third party organization. This "outside organization" manages and proves the authenticity of the keys used in the system. The third party company has to protect the public keys and provide the correct ones to authorized cryptosystem members.

Because of the pros and cons of both encryption methods, business organizations combine them to create safer and practical security systems. Most of these businesses are in the communications and information technology industries.

Here's the list of asymmetric algorithms:

1. RSA (Rivest- Shamir – Adleman) Asymmetric algorithms

RSA is one of the first practical public key cryptosystems. It is used for secure data transcription. The encryption key is public, but the decryption key is private. The RSA user can create and publish a public key to encrypt a message. MIT owns the patent for RSA.

The RSA algorithm has four steps:

- Key distribution
- Key generation
- Encryption
- Decryption

As mentioned earlier, RSA has a public encryption key and a private decryption key. The underlying principle behind RSA is the fact that it's quite practical to large positive integers such as n, d, and e with modular exponentiation (m). It's illustrated as:

$$(m^e)^d \mod n = m$$

Even when you know the values for m, n, and e, it is still difficult to find d. In some operations, the order can be modified such as it appears like this:

$$(m^d)^e \mod n = m$$

The public keys (e, n) can be transmitted to reliable but public route. The private key (d), on the other hand is never revealed to anyone. Once the key is distributed to other users, it can be used over and over.

But how do you encrypt a data using RSA? Well, let's say that Kate wants to send the data M to Edward. She first turns M into an integer "m" such as that

$0 \leq m < n$ and that gcd (m, n) =1 by using a reversible protocol called padding scheme. Then, Kate computed the ciphertext "c"using Edward's public key "e". So, it looks like this:

$$c \equiv m^e \mod n$$

This algorithm can be done efficiently using modular exponentiation even for 500 bit numbers. After the encryption, Kate can transmit "c" or the ciphertext to Edward.

To decrypt the message, Alice can recover "m" from "c" using the private key exponent "d" using the formula:

$$c^d \equiv (m^e)^d \equiv m \mod n$$

So, to recover the M (original message), she needs to revert m to M by reversing the padding scheme.

To generate a key, you can use OPENSSL. You can also generate a key by writing a code in JavaScript.

You can also use RSA to sign a message. This way, the recipient can verify the identity of the sender.

2. Deffie Hellman

Deffie Hellman is a method of exchanging cryptographic keys securely over a public channel. This is also called as the exponential key exchange. This scheme was created by Martin Hellman and Whitfield Diffie in 1976. This algorithm uses p or prime - a multiplicative group of integers modulo. This algorithm also uses g which is the primitive root modulo p. The values of p and g are chosen in a way that it can take any value from p-1 to 1.

This protocol is considered as secured against eavesdroppers. Deffie-Helman key exchange is a great defense against mass surveillance. It is the cornerstone of cryptography that's used for HTTPS web sites, VPNs, email, and other protocols.

3. Digital Signature Algorithm

The DSA or the Digital Signature Algorithm is a processing standard set by the Federal Government for digital signatures. The DSA was proposed by the NIST or National Institute of Standards and Technology. This algorithm is patented under a former NSA employee named David W. Kravitz. The patent was given to the United States Government so programmers and cryptographers can use this for free.

The DSA key generation has two phases – parameter generation and per-user keys.

You have to choose a cryptographic hash function H. H was always SHA-1 in the original DSS. But, the current DSS now uses the string SHA-2 hash function. After choosing a cryptographic hash function, you need to choose your key length. The length is the major determinant of how strong your key is.

It is recommended to opt for 3072 key length if you want the security lifetime of your key to last beyond 2030. After choosing the key length, you also need to pick an N-bit prime q, and then pick an L-bit prime modulus p where $p-1$ will be a multiple of q. Then, pick g – a figure whose modulo p is q. You can achieve this if you set $g = h^{(p-1)/q} \bmod p$ for some arbitrary h ($1 < h < p-1$).

Then, given the parameters that you have set, you can now compute for your public or private key.

4. ElGamal

ElGamal encryption is an algorithm that's based on Diffie- Hellman key exchange. It was developed in 1985 by Taher Elgamal. This encryption algorithm is used by recent PGP versions, free GNU privacy guard software, and other cryptosystems. This encryption is defined over cyclic group G. In algebra, this is a group that's generated by a single element. The element G is the generator of the group. The security of the encryption depends upon the level of difficulty in computing G. The more difficult the problem is, the more secure the encryption is. This encryption has 3 components, namely:

- Key generator – You need to generate an efficient description of G (the cyclic group) of Q (order) using g (generator). You need to choose exponent randomly from 1 to q-1. Here's the formula:

$$h := g^x$$

  H is the key, g is the generator and x is the exponent . X can come randomly from 1 to q-1. After computing for the value of the key, you can publish H along with the description (G, Q, g). H, along with the description, becomes the public key. X, on the other hand, is your private key and must be kept a secret.

- Encryption Algorithm

  To encrypt the message (M), you need to use your public key (h,G,Q,g).

- DecryptionAlgorithm

  To decrypt the ciphertext (C1, C2), you'll need to use the private key X.

This algorithm is used in hybrid cryptosystem. The security of this encryption depends on the cyclic group G and the padding scheme on the message.

5. ECDSA

ECDSA or Elliptic Curve Digital Signature Algorithm uses elliptic curve cryptography. ECDSA private key is used to sign software for the Sony PlayStation 3.

6. XTR

XTR is an effective public key based on 3rd order LFSR (linear feedback shift register). XTR is the first cryptographical method that uses GF(p 2) arithmetic to attain the GF(p 6) security. The use of XTR in cryptographic protocols brings so much savings both in computational and communication overhead.

Kerckhoff's Principle

During the 19th century, a Dutch cryptographer named Auguste Kerckhoff identified the requirements of a reliable cryptosystem. He stated that a cryptosystem must be secure even if everything related to it – except the keys – are available to the public. In addition, Mr. Kerckhoff established six principles in designing new cryptosystems. These principles are:

1. The cryptosystem needs to be unbreakable (i.e. in a practical sense). This excludes the system's vulnerability to mathematical intrusions.

2. The system should be secure enough that members can still use it even during an attack from unauthorized entities. The cryptosystem needs to allow authorized members to do what they need to do.

3. The keys used in the system must be easy to change, memorize, and communicate.

4. The resulting ciphertexts must be transmissible by unsecure channels such as telegraph.

5. The documents and devices used in the encryption system must be portable and easy to operate.

6. Lastly, the system must be user-friendly. It should not require high IQ or advanced memorization skills.

Modern cryptographers refer to the second rule as the Kerckhoff principle. They apply it in almost all encryption algorithms (e.g. AES, DES, etc.). Experts in this field consider these algorithms to be completely secure. In addition, these experts believe that the security of the transmitted message relies exclusively on the protection given to the private encryption keys used.

Maintaining the confidentiality of the encryption and decryption algorithms may prove to be a difficult problem. Actually, you can only keep these algorithms secret if you will share them with a few individuals.

Today, cryptography must meet the needs of internet users. Since more and more people gain access to hacking information and advanced computers, keeping an algorithm secret is extremely difficult. That means you should always use the principles given by Kerckhoff in designing your own cryptosystems.

Chapter 4: Different Types of Attacks on Cryptosystems

Nowadays, almost every aspect of human life is affected by information. Thus, it is necessary to safeguard important data from the intrusions of unauthorized parties. These intrusions (also called attacks) are usually classified based on the things done by the intruder. Currently, attacks are classified into two types: passive attacks and active attacks.

Passive Attacks

Passive attacks are designed to establish unauthorized access to certain pieces of information. For instance, activities such as data interception and tapping on a communication channel are considered as passive attacks.

These activities are inherently passive: they do not attempt to modify the message or destroy the channel of communication. They simply want to "steal" (i.e. see) the information being transmitted. Compared to stealing physical items, stealing data allows the legitimate owner (i.e. the receiver) to possess the information after the attack. It is important to note that passive data attacks are more harmful than stealing of physical items, since data theft may be unnoticed by the receiver.

Active Attacks

Active attacks are meant to alter or eliminate the information being sent. Here are some examples:

- Unauthorized modification of the message.

- Triggering unauthorized transmission of data.

- Modification of the data used for authentication purposes (e.g. timestamp, sender's information, etc.).

- Unauthorized removal of information.

- Preventing authorized people from accessing the information. This is known as "denial of service."

Modern cryptography arms people with the tools and methods for preventing the attacks explained above.

The Assumptions of a Cryptosystem Attacker

This section of the book will discuss two important things about system attacks: (1) cryptosystem environments and (2) the attacks used by unauthorized parties to infiltrate cryptosystems.

The Cryptosystem Environment

Before discussing the types of data attacks, it is important to understand the environment of cryptosystems. The intruder's knowledge and assumptions about this factor greatly influence his choices of possible attacks.

In the field of cryptography, three assumptions are made about the attacker and the cryptosystem itself. These assumptions are:

1. Information about the Encryption Method – Cryptosystem developers base their projects on two kinds of algorithms:

    i.   Public Algorithms – These algorithms share information with the public.

    ii. Proprietary Algorithms – These algorithms keep the details of the cryptosystem within the organization. Only the users and designers can access information about the algorithm.

    When using a proprietary (or private) algorithm, cryptographers obtain security through obscurity. In general, these are developed by people within the organization and are not thoroughly checked for weaknesses. Thus, private algorithms may have loopholes that intruders can exploit.

    In addition, private algorithms limit the number of people that can join the system. You can't use them for modern communication. You should also remember Kerckoff's principle: "The encryption and decryption keys hold the security of the entire cryptosystem. The algorithms involved can be shared with the public."

    Thus, the first assumption is: "The attacker knows the encryption and decryption algorithms."

2. Obtainability of the Ciphertext – The ciphertext (i.e. the encrypted information) is transmitted through unsecured public channels. Because of this the second assumption is: "The attacker can access ciphertexts created by the cryptosystem."

3. Obtainability of the Ciphertext and the Plaintext – This assumption is more obscure than the previous one. In some situations, the attacker may obtain both the plaintext and the ciphertext. Here are some sample scenarios:

i.   The attacker convinces the sender to encrypt certain pieces of information and gets the resulting ciphertext.

ii.   The recipient may share the decrypted information with the attacker. The attacker obtains the corresponding ciphertext from the communication channel used.

iii.   The attacker may create pairs of plaintexts and ciphertexts using the encryption key. Since the encryption key is in the public domain, potential attackers can access it easily. It's a "hit and miss" type of tactic.

Cryptographic Attacks

Obviously, every attacker wants to break into the cryptosystem and obtain the plaintext. To fulfill this objective, the attacker simply needs to identify the decryption key. Obtaining the algorithms is easy since the information is available publicly.

This means the attacker focuses on obtaining the secret decryption key. Once he/she gets this information, the cryptosystem is broken (or compromised).

Cryptographic attacks are divided into several categories. These are:

- BFA (Brute Force Attack) – Here, the intruder tries to find the decryption key by entering all possible information. For instance, the key contains 8 bits. That means the total number of possible keys is 256 (i.e. 2^8). The attacker tries all of these keys in order to obtain the plaintext. The longer the key, the longer the time needed for successful decryption.

- COA (Ciphertext Only Attack) – This tactic requires the complete set of ciphertexts used for a message. When COA gets the plaintext from the given ciphertexts, the tactic is considered successful. Attackers may also get the corresponding encryption key using this attack.

- CPA (Chosen Plaintext Attack) – This attack requires the attacker to work on the plaintext he/she selected for encryption. Simply put, the attacker has the plaintext-ciphertext combination. It means the task of decrypting the information is easy and simple. It is the first part of the attack – convincing the sender to encrypt certain pieces of information – that presents the most difficulties.

- KPA (Known Plaintext Attack) – With this tactic, the attacker should know some parts of the plaintext. He/she has to use this knowledge to obtain the rest of the message.

- Birthday Attack – This is a subtype of the brute force approach. Attackers use this tactic when working against cryptographic hash functions. Once the intruder finds two inputs that produce similar values, a collision is said to occur: the hash function is broken and the system is breached.

This attack is based on the Birthday Paradox -- that if there are around twenty three people in a room, the odds are around 50% of that two of those people share the same birth date.

For example, Kate in in the room with twenty three people and has twenty two chances of sharing a birthday with anyone else. If Kate fails to find a match, she leaves and then Edwa44rd has 21 chances to share a birthday with someone else. Then, if he fails to match, then Albert has twenty chances and so on. If you do the math, 22 pairs, plus 21, plus 20, plus 19, plus 18, plus 17, plus 16, plus 15, plus 14, plus 13, plus 12, plus 11, plus 10, plus 9, plus 8, plus 7, plus 6, plus 5, plus 4, plus 3, plus 2, and plus 1 is equal to 253 pairs. Each of these 254 pairs have 1 out of 365 chance of having the same birthday. The odds of the match are more than 50% at two hundred fifty three pairs.

The birthday attack is often used to find out collisions in hash functions such as SHA1 and MD5.

- MIM Attack (Man in the Middle Attack) – This attack is particularly designed for public key cryptosystems. In general, these systems require the exchange of keys before the actual transmission of the ciphertext. Here is an example:

  o Member1 wants to send a message to Member2. To do this, he sends a request for Member2's public key.

  o An intruder blocks the request and sends his own public key.

  o Thus, the unauthorized party acquires the information that will be sent by Member1.

  o To avoid detection, the intruder encrypts the data again and sends it to Member2.

      o The intruder uses his own public key. That means Member2 will see the attacker's key instead of Member1's.

- SCA (Side Channel Attack) – This attack is used to exploit the weaknesses of a cryptosystem's physical implementation. Here, the attackers ignore the system's algorithms and digital protection.

- Fault Analysis Attacks – When using this attack, the intruder looks for errors produced by the system. He/she uses the resulting information to breach the system's defenses.

- Timing Attacks – Here, attackers use the fact that different calculations require different processing times. These people can acquire some data about the message processed by a computer system. They do this by measuring the time used by the computer in performing its calculations.

- Power Analysis Attacks – These attacks are similar to the previous one. However, instead of time, they use the amount of power consumed by the computer system. This information is used to determine the nature of the plaintext.

An Important Note About Cryptographic Attacks

The attacks explained above are theoretical and highly academic. Actually, most of those attacks are defined by cryptography instructors. Some of the attacks you read about involve unrealistic assumptions about the attacker and/or the system's environment.

However, these attacks have excellent potential. Attackers may find ways to improve them. It would be great if you will still consider these attacks when designing your own cryptosystems.

Cryptology Protocols

The internet was initially designed only for a few people. But, when people found out about this amazing new technology, they want to be part of it. In the 1990s, the use of computers increased and internet actually became accessible to almost anyone. Because the internet was created for just a few people, the code protocol used to build the Internet called TCPIP does not have intrinsic security measures. This means that the message is sent in plain text. Anyone can read the transmitted information by using a certain device. You also cannot verify if the "sender" is the real sender. Also, with the original TCPIP design, there's no way to determine if the data has been intercepted and modified while in transit. The

TCPIP was merely designed to make sure that the data goes where it's supposed to go. But luckily, experts have invented several solutions to this security problem. These solutions are called cryptology protocols. There are a number of cryptology protocols available today, including:

1. Internet Protocol Security or IPsec is a security suite that is used for securing IP communications. IPsec works by encrypting information through encapsulation. It works at the network layer of the Open System Interconnection or OSI model. IPsec has three goals:

   - Authentication – Ipsec verifies the identity of both the sender and the claimer.

   - Integrity – Ipsec ensures that the contents of the packet are not changed during the transit.

   - Confidentiality – Ipsec protects the content of the message through encryption.

   IPsec provides an automated solution to the authentication, integrity, and confidentiality problems.

   To understand how IPsec works, it's important to understand the structure of an ordinary IP packet. An ordinary IP packet contains the information that you want to send on a specific network. Then, it contains a "TCP header". The "TCP Header" wraps the information and it selects the destination of the message. So, basically, it is more of a layered structure. Then, the IP header wraps the TCP header. The IP header is in charge of transporting the information from the sender to the receiver. Once the IP packet reaches the receiving network, it will be removed. Now, the IP header will deliver the message to the recipient within the receiving network. Once the true receiver receives the information, the TCP header will be removed.

   The difference between IPsec and regular IP is that the IPsec starts out with information wrapped around the TCP header. Then, the TCP header is wrapped by the IPsec header. Lastly, the IP header encapsulates the IPsec header. A regular IP packet looks like this:

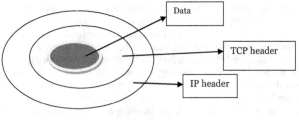

The IPsec architecture, on the other hand, looks like this:

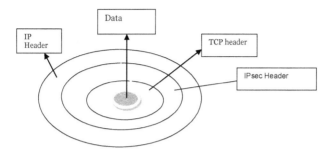

IPsec headers may include encryption, but it can also include authentication protocols.

2. SSL or Secure Sockets Layer

SSL keeps your information secure in two ways. First, let's say that you are in a coffee shop and you are using a public wifi. Without SSL, another user can easily steal your data because you are on a public network.

SSL is a security technology that's used for establishing an encrypted link between a browser and a web server. This encrypted link ensures that information is passed between the browsers and the web server remain integral and private.

SSL is considered as the industry standard. It is used by many e-commerce websites to protect their online transactions with their clients. SSL allows the secure transmission of confidential information such as social security numbers and banking log in credentials.. Without SSL, the data sent between web servers and browsers are sent in plain text. This makes the website vulnerable to eavesdropping. An attacker can easily intercept all the information sent between a browser and a server so they can see and use all of this information.

This security protocol is used by millions of people. SSL provides state-of-the-art data encryption. It also has over 99% browser compatibility.

3. PGP – PGP is also known as Pretty Good Privacy. It is a data decryption and encryption program that provides authentication and cryptography privacy for data communication. This was created by Phil Zimmerman.

PGP uses a serial combination of data compression, hashing, public-key cryptography, and symmetric cryptography. PGP is used to send information and messages privately. So, it combines the public key encryption with the symmetric key encryption. This security protocol encrypts the data using a symmetric encryption algorithm. You'll need a symmetric key to do this. Each key is called session key because it is only used once. The session key and the data are sent to the receiver. The receiver should use the session key to decrypt the message. But, the public key is used to protect the information during transmission.

4. SSH – SSH or Secure Socket Shell is a security protocol and a command interface that's used for getting secured access to a computer. This protocol is used by various network administrators to control the servers remotely. The SSH suite has three utilities – SSH, SLOGIN, and SCP. SSH uses public keys for both authentication and connection. It uses encryption algorithms such as Blowfish, IDEA, and DES.

SSH protects the network from attacks such as IP source routing, IP spoofing, and DNS spoofing.

5. Kerberos – Kerberos is an authentication protocol that's designed to provide strong authentication by using secret-key cryptography. This protocol was created by MIT as a solution to various security problems. This protocol uses strong cryptography to facilitate authentication in an insecure network.

Attacks are common, but it can be avoided. So, try your best to use a strong cryptographic algorithm. Also, several security protocols are available to protect your system from cryptographic attacks.

Chapter 5: Traditional Cryptography

You have learned about the basics of modern cryptography. You also discovered the different tools that you can use in designing your own cryptosystems. One of the powerful tools at your disposal is the symmetric key encryption: a mode of encryption that uses a single key for the entire communication process.

This chapter will discuss this mode further so you will know how to apply it in developing cryptosystems.

Old Cryptographic Systems

At this point, you have to study the cryptosystems used in the ancient times. These "old systems" share similar characteristics, which are:

- These cryptosystems are based on the symmetric mode of encryption.

- The message is protected using a single tool: confidentiality.

- These systems use alphabets to facilitate encryption. In contrast, modern cryptosystems use digital data and binary numbers to encrypt a message.

These old systems are called "ciphers." Basically, a cipher is just a group of procedures performed in order to encrypt and decrypt data. You may think of these procedures as the "algorithms" of these ancient cryptosystems.

<u>1. The Caesar Cipher</u>

This cipher is based on a single alphabet. Here, you can create a ciphertext just by replacing every letter of the message with a different one. Cryptologists consider this cipher as the simplest scheme today.

The Caesar Cipher is also called "shift cipher," since each letter is shifted by a fixed number. If you are using the English alphabet, you can use the numbers from 0 to 25. The people involved must choose a certain "shift number" before encoding the plaintext. The number will serve as the encryption and decryption key for the entire communication process.

<u>How to Use the Shift Cipher</u>

1. The sender and the receiver select a shift number.

2. The sender writes down the alphabet twice (i.e. a-z followed by a-z).

3. That person gets the plaintext and finds the appropriate letters. However, he moves the letters based on the shift number selected. For example, if

they are using the number 1, he will replace the letter "A"s with "B"s, the "B"s with "C"s, and so on.

4. The encryption procedure is done once all of the letters have been shifted.

5. The sender transmits the ciphertext to the receiver.

6. The receiver moves the letters of the ciphertext backwards, depending on the shift number being used.

7. Once all of the letters have been shifted, the decryption process is completed. The receiver can use the information he received from the sender.

The Cipher's Security Value

This is not a secure system since the possible encryption keys are extremely limited. If you are using the English alphabet, your possible keys are restricted to 25. This number is not enough for those who need more security. In this situation, an attacker may acquire your key just by carrying out a thorough key search.

2. The Simple Substitution Cipher

This is an improved version of the Caesar Cipher. Instead of using numbers to determine the ciphertext, you will choose your own equivalent for each letter of the alphabet. For instance, "A.C... X.Z" and "Z.X... C.A" are two simple permutations of the letters in the English alphabet.

Since this alphabet has 26 letters, the total permutations can be derived through this formula: $4x10^{26}$. The people involved can select any of these permutations to create the ciphertext. The permutation scheme serves as the key for this cryptosystem.

How to Use this Cipher

1. Write down the letters from A to Z.

2. The involved parties choose a permutation for each letter. For example, they might replace the "A"s with "F"s, the "B" with "W", etc. These new letters don't need to have any logical or mathematical relationship with the letter they represent.

3. The sender encrypts the plaintext using the selected permutations.

4. The message is sent to the receiver.

5. The receiver decodes the ciphertext using the chosen permutations.

The Cipher's Security Value

This cipher is way much stronger than the Caesar Cipher. Even strong computer systems cannot decode the ciphertext since the possible permutations (i.e. 4×10^{26}) are too many. Cryptosystems based on this cipher can stop attackers that rely on a brute force approach. However, this substitution system is based on a simple scheme. In fact, attackers have succeeded in breaking letter permutations in the past.

The Monoalphabetic and Polyalphabetic Ciphers

Monoalphabetic Ciphers are ciphers that rely on a single encryption system. In other words, a single encryption alphabet is used for each "normal" alphabet throughout the entire communication process. For instance, if "C" is encoded as "X", "C" must be written as "X" each time it appears in the plaintext.

The two encryption systems discussed above belong to this type.

Polyalphabetic Ciphers, on the other hand, involve multiple encryption alphabets. The encryption alphabets may be switched at different segments of the encryption procedure. Here are two examples of polyalphabetic ciphers:

The Playfair Cipher

This encryption scheme uses pairs of letters to create encryption alphabets. Here, the people involved must create a table where letters are written down. The table used is a 5x5 square (i.e. 25 in total): the squares inside the table hold the letters of the alphabet. Since there are 26 letters in the English alphabet, a letter must be omitted. Cryptographers often omit the letter "J" when using this cipher.

The sender and the receiver must choose a certain keyword, say "lessons." They must write this keyword in the key table, from left to right. In addition, they should not repeat letters. Once the word is written down, the sender/receiver must complete the table using the unused letters (i.e. alphabetically arranged). With the word "lessons" as the keyword and J omitted, the key table should look like this:

L	E	S	O	N
A	B	C	D	F
G	H	I	K	M
P	Q	R	T	U
V	W	X	Y	Z

How to Use this Cipher

1. You should split the message into diagraphs (i.e. pairs of letters). If the total number of letters is an odd number, you should add a Z to the last letter. As an example, let's encrypt the word "human" using the key table created above. It will look like this:

HU MA NZ

2. Here are the encryption rules:

   a. If both letters are in the same column, you should use the letter under each one. You have to go back to the top if you are using the bottom letter. In our example, N and Z are in the same column. Thus, this pair becomes FN.

   b. If both letters are placed in the same row, use the letter located at the right of each one. You need to go back to the first letter of the row if you are working on the rightmost letter. (This rule doesn't apply to our example.)

   c. If none of the previous rules apply, create a rectangle using the pair of letters. Afterward, use the letters on the opposite corner of the correct letters. Work on the letters horizontally. According to this rule, the HU pair is converted to MQ (look at the key table). MA, on the other hand, becomes GF.

3. Using these rules, the word "human" becomes MQ GF FN when encrypted using the Playfair Cipher.

4. You just have to reverse the process if you want to decrypt the message.

<u>The Playfair Cipher's Security Value</u>

This scheme is stronger than the systems discussed earlier. Attackers will have a difficult time analyzing all of the possible keys. In general, cryptologists use this cipher to protect important information. Lots of people rely on the Playfair Cipher since it is easy to use and doesn't require special tools.

<u>*The Vigenere Cipher*</u>

This encryption scheme uses a word (also known as text string) as the key. This key is used to change the plaintext. For instance, let's use the word "human" as the key. You should convert each letter into its numeric value (i.e. A = 1, B = 2, etc.). In our example:

H = 8, U = 21, M = 13, A = 1, N = 14

<u>How to Use this Cipher</u>

1. If you want to encrypt "cold water," you have to write the letters down. Then, write the key numbers (i.e. 8, 21, 13, 1, and 14) under the words, one number for each letter. Repeat the numbers as necessary. It looks like this:

C	O	L	D	W	A	T	E	R
8	21	`13	1	14	8	21	13	1

2. Shift the letters of the normal alphabet according to the number written on the table. Here it is:

C	O	L	D	W	A	T	E	R
8	21	13	1	14	8	21	13	1
K	J	Y	E	K	I	O	R	S

3. As you can see, each letter of the plaintext is moved by a different amount – the amount is specified by the key. The letters of your key should be less than or equal to that of your message.

4. To decrypt the message, you just have to use the same key and shift the letters backward.

<u>The Vigenere Cipher's Security Value</u>

This cipher offers excellent security: better than the three ciphers discussed above. Cryptographers use this encryption system to protect military and political data. Because of its apparent invulnerability, security experts call this the "unbreakable cipher."

Chapter 6: Modern Cryptography Schemes

Nowadays, cryptographers use digital data to establish encryption systems. This data is often represented as sets of binary digits (also called "bits"). Modern cryptosystems must process these binary strings to create more strings. Symmetric encryption techniques are categorized based on the procedures performed on the digital information. These categories are:

Block Ciphers

These ciphers group the digital data into separate blocks and process them one at a time. The number of bits contained in a data block is predetermined and unchangeable. Two popular block ciphers, AES and DES, have block sizes of 128 and 64, respectively.

In general, a block cipher uses a set of plaintext data and produces a set of ciphertext data, usually of the same size. Once the block size is assigned, it can no longer be modified. The block size used for the system doesn't affect the strength of encryption techniques involved. The strength of this cipher relies on the length of its key.

Block Size

Although you can use any block size, there are some things you have to consider when working on this aspect of your cryptosystem. These are:

- Avoid small block sizes – Let's assume that a block size is equal to m. Here, the total number of possible plaintext combinations is 2^m. If an intruder acquires the plaintext data used for previous messages, he/she can initiate a "dictionary attack" against your cryptosystem. Dictionary attacks are performed by creating a dictionary of ciphertext and plaintext pairs generated using an encryption key. You should remember this simple rule: the smaller the block size, the weaker the system is against dictionary attacks.

- Don't use extremely large block sizes – Large block sizes mean more processing time for your computer system. Cryptographers working on large bit sizes experience efficiency issues. Often, the plaintext must be padded in order to get the desired block size.

- Use a block size that is a multiple of 8 – Computers can easily handle binary digits that are multiples of 8. You can take advantage of this fact by choosing a block size that has this mathematical property.

Different Types of Block Cipher Schemes

Cryptographers use a variety of block cipher encryption schemes in their systems. Here are some of the most popular block ciphers being used today:

- AES (Advanced Encryption Standard) – This cipher is based on Rijndael, an award-winning encryption algorithm. You have three choices (128-bit, 192-bit, or 256-bit) in choosing the key length for both decryption and encryption. The result of this encryption can be downloaded in a text file.

- IDEA (International Data Encryption Algorithm) – This is considered as one of the strongest ciphers available. Its block size is equal to 64 while its key size is equal to 128 bits. Many applications utilize this encryption. For instance, the old versions of PGP (Pretty Good Privacy) protocol used IDEA extensively. Because of patent issues, the utilization of this encryption scheme is restricted.

- This algorithm was previously known as IPES or Improved Proposed Encryption Standard. This was designed by Xuejia Lai and James Massey. This algorithm was designed to replace DES. In 1996, well-known cryptographer Bruce Schneider said that he thought that IDEA is the best and most secure block cipher algorithm at that time. But, by 1999, Schneider no longer recommends the use of IDEA because of the proliferation of faster and more complex algorithms. IDEA was broken in 2011 and 2012 using a narrow-bicliques attack.

- Lucifer – This is a block cipher designed by German cryptographer Horst Feistel. This was created in 1971 and it is the direct pre-cursor of DES or Digital Encryption Standard. This algorithm is used in the 1970s for electronic banking.

- DES (Digital Encryption Standard) – This is the most popular block cipher during the 1990s. Because of their small size, DES ciphers are now considered as "broken ciphers."

- RC2 – We have discussed RC2 earlier as it is one of the assymetric ciphers. This cipher uses the block cipher scheme. This was designed in 1987. The RC2 algorithm was kept a secret but in 1996, an anonymous user posted the source code of RC2 on the Usenet forum. According to John Kelsey, an NIST cryptographer, RC2 is vulnerable to related key attack using 2^{34} plaintext.

- Blowfish – As discussed earlier, Blowfish is a symmetric-key block cipher designed by Bruce Schneier. It has good encryption rate but today, AES is much more preferred than Blowfish. This block cipher has amazing speed but it is vulnerable to attacks especially if it has weak keys.

- Intel Cascaded Cipher – This high band-width cipher is based on AES and it was designed by Gary Graunke and Ernie Brickell. This cipher was used as an optional component of Microsoft Vista's Output Content Protection scheme.

Stream Ciphers

With this scheme, the information is encrypted one binary digit at a time. The resulting ciphertext is equivalent to the data processed (e.g. 10 bits of plaintext produce 10 bits of ciphertext). Basically, stream ciphers are block ciphers with a block size limit of 1 bit.

Stream ciphers are only used with symmetric encryption. Encryption is done one bit or byte at the a time. This cipher usually use low hardware complexity. You do not have to do fancy calculations to encrypt using stream ciphers so this could be done quickly.

What the algorithm does is that it generates a key stream which is a combination of 1s and 0s. Those bits are going to be processed using the XOR (exclusive or) operation.
So, here's how it looks like:

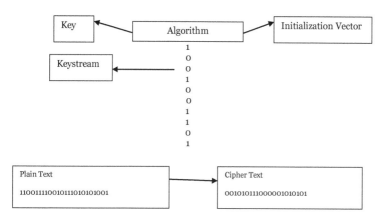

The message is in binary so the first bit that comes out of the keystream is XOR-ed (using the "exclusive or" operation) to the first bit in your plain text message. Each bit that comes from the stream cipher is converted into the cipher text.

When encrypting using stream ciphers, the initialization vector or IV should never be the same when you're starting to do other streams. Otherwise, someone may figure out that IV or initialization vector that you're using and the key and the cipher that's being used. That person may apply it every time you send data across the network. To maintain maximum security, you have to make sure that your IV is always changing each time you use stream ciphers to encrypt a message or information.

Here are the different types of stream ciphers:

1. Synchronous Stream Ciphers

In this type of stream ciphers, a stream of pseudo random digits is generated independently. Then, it's combined with plain text during encryption or the ciphertext during the decryption process. The binary digits are used as plain text and keystream. The keystream is then mixed with the plaintext using the XOR operation. The combined plaintext and keystream is called a binary additive stream cipher.

In synchronous stream cipher, it is important that the digits remain intact during transmission. If a digit is removed or added during transmission, the decryption will not be successful as the synchronization is lost.

2. Self-synchronization Stream Ciphers

This approach uses a number of the previous N ciphertext digits to calculate the keystream.

Stream ciphers are frequently used because of their speed. Here are some of the other benefits of stream ciphers:

- Stream ciphers are faster than block ciphers.

- Bytes are individually encrypted.

- Stream ciphers are easier to implement.

However, stream ciphers also have limitations and disadvantage. Stream ciphers are difficult to implement correctly. This is because the keystream has strict requirements. Stream ciphers also do not provide authentication or integrity protection. So, the data or message is less secure.

There are a number of stream ciphers that are available. Some of which were discussed earlier:

- ABC – This cipher was developed by Andre Bogdanov, Vladimir Anashin, Sandeep Kumar, and IIya Kizhvatov.

- MAG – This is a stream cipher algorithm created by Rade Vuckovac.

- NLS – This stream cipher algorithm was designed by Australian developer and businessman, Gregory Rose.

- Polar Bear – This algorithm was designed by Mas Naslund and Johan Hastad.

- Rabbit – Rabbit was created in 2003 by Martin Boesgaard, Thomas Pedersen, Ove Scavenius, and Mette Vesterager. This algorithm is known for its high speed. The Rabbit algorithm uses a 64 bit initialization vector and a 128 key bit key. This algorithm was designed for high speed software. Rabbit has a 128-bit security against attackers who target a specific key. But, it only has 96-bit security from attackers who target different keys at once.

- ORYX – This encryption algorithm is used in cellular networks to protect data traffic. This stream cipher have a strong 96 bit key strength.

- Panama – This is a cryptography that can be used both as a stream cipher and hash function. This was developed and presented in 1998 by Craig Clapp and Joan Daemen.

- FISH (Fibonacci Shrinking) is a stream cipher that uses Lagged Fibonacci generators. As the name suggests, it also incorporates the use of shrinking generator cipher. This algorithm was developed and published by Siemens in 1993.

- Rambutan – This is a family of encryption technologies that are created by CESG (Communications Electronics Security Group) – the technical arm of the secret communications agency of the United Kingdom. This cipher has 5 shift registers. Each shift register has 80 bits. Rambutan also has a 112-bit key size.

- Sober-128 – This is a synchronous stream cipher designed in 2003 by Hawkes and Rose. This cipher has a 128-bit key length. In 2004, Japanese scientists found out that there's a 2^{-6} probability that an attack can forge a message.

- Hermes 8- This stream cipher algorithm was developed by Ulrich Kaiser.

- QUAD – This is a new stream cipher. This was designed by Henri Gilbert, Come Berbain, and Jacques Patarin in 2006 at Eurocrypt. This cryptography has an 80-bit sizes.

- LILI-128 – This is a synchronous stream cipher developed in 2000. This was presented during the New European Schemes for Signatures, Integrity, and Encryption research convention. This cipher is easy to implement in both hardware and software. This cipher was unfortunately broken in 2007 in only 1.61 hours.

- Solitaire – This cryptographic algorithm was created an American cryptographer named Bruce Schneider. This algorithm allows field agents to communicate to each other securely without relying on electronics and other incriminating devices.

- Trivium – This is a synchronous stream cipher that's designed to provide a flexible trade off between gate count and speed. This algorithm was developed by Bart Preneel and Christophe De Canniere.

- CryptMT – This stream cipher uses the pseudo-random number generator called Mersenne Twister. This algorithm was developed by Japanese cryptographers Hagita Mariko, Makoto Matsumoto, Matsuo Saito, and Takuji Nishimura.

- Salsa20 – This stream cipher was designed by American-German cryptographer Daniel J. Bernstein. This algorithm was built on a pseudo-random function that's based on ARX or add-rotate-xor operations. Salsa20 has a 265-bit key, a 64-bit stream, and a 64-bit nonce (arbitrary number). This cipher has a speed of four to fourteen cycles per byte on modern x86 processors. This cipher is not patented so it can be used by anyone. Bernstein created a related cipher in 2008 called ChaCha.

- Edon80 – This stream cipher algorithm is designed by Smile Markovski, Danilo Gligoroski, Marjan Gusev, and Ljupco Koracev.

- Wake – This stream cipher was designed in 1993 by David Wheeler. Wake stands for Word Auto Key Encryption. This cipher generates the keystream from previous ciphertext blocks. Wake is fast, but vulnerable to attacks.

- SOSEMANUK – This is a cipher developed by Olivier Billet, Come Berbain, Nicolas Courtois, Anne Canteaut, Aline Gouget, Cedrix Lauradoux, Herve Sibert, and Thomas Pornin. The key length of this cipher can vary from 128 to 256 bits. But, the guaranteed security is only 128 bits.

- Grain – This cipher was developed in 2004 by Thomas Johansson, Martin Hell, and Willi Meier. This was designed primarily for restricted hardware environments. It has a 64-bit IV and 80-bit key.

- ISAAC (Indirection, Shift, Accumulate, Add, and Count) – This is a cryptologically secure stream cipher and pseudorandom number generator. This was designed in 1996 by an American computer professional named Robert J. Jenkins Jr. This algorithm is a bit similar to RC4 and it uses a wide array of two hundred fifty six four-octet integers.

- Pike – This is an improvised version of FISH. It was designed by a well-known British security engineer named Ross John Anderson. Pike is ten percent faster than FISH and it is cryptographically stronger. No attacks has been published and it has a huge key length.

- Mickey (Mutual Irregular Clocking Keystream Generator) – This stream algorithm was developed by Matthew Dodd and Steve Babbage. This cipher has a variable initialization vector length from 0 to 80 bits. It also has an 80-bit key length.

So, which one is better – stream cipher or block cipher? Well, each has its own advantage and disadvantage. Stream ciphers are best when the amount of data is unknown. On the other hand, block ciphers are best if the amount of data is known ahead of time such as HTTP, file, or data fields. This algorithm was designed for high speed software.

Chapter 7: The Pros and Cons of Cryptography

This chapter will discuss the pros and cons of using cryptography.

The Pros

Today, security experts consider cryptography as one of their most useful tools. It provides four things needed for modern communication:

1. Authentication – Cryptographic techniques like digital signatures prevent spoofing and data forgeries.

2. Confidentiality – Encryption schemes protect information from unauthorized parties.

3. Non-repudiation – The digital signatures used in cryptography prove the identity of the sender. Thus, disputes regarding this factor are prevented.

4. Data Integrity – Cryptography involves hash functions that can maintain the integrity of the data being transmitted.

The Cons

Nothing is perfect. Here are the problems associated with cryptography:

- Legitimate users may encounter issues when accessing well-encrypted information. This can turn into a disaster if a certain piece of information has to be obtained quickly.

- Constant availability of information – a basic aspect of communications and information technology – is hard to secure when using cryptography.

- Cryptosystems prevent selective access control. Some organizations need to provide exclusive file access to certain officers. When using cryptosystems, these organizations will have problems in giving selective access to their chosen members. This is because cryptosystems apply the same security measures on every file.

Chapter 8: Uses of Cryptography and Laws that Govern the Use and Transfer of Cryptographic Technologies

Millions of e-commerce data crisscross the internet daily, but all this data is not safe without some very important numbers. These numbers are called prime numbers. Prime numbers have long fascinated mathematicians. It helps keep data confidential. It also aids the authentication process and it helps keep data integrity. But, what types of institutions use cryptography?

1.   E-commerce Sites

E-commerce sites typically use key codes and cryptography to authenticate the identity of their buyers. They also use these key codes to protect the financial information of their clients. It guards the information from cyber criminals and fraudulent individuals.

Account money systems such as e-gold and PayPal are protected by a cryptographic protocol called SSL which we have discussed earlier in this book.

E-commerce sites use what we call financial cryptography. Financial cryptography is significantly different from traditional cryptography, which is usually used for military intelligence purposes. Financial cryptography is a combination of seven disciplines:

- Software engineering
- Governance
- Accounting
- Rights
- Cryptography
- Value
- Financial Institutions

2. Government Organizations

It is no secret that government organizations, particularly the military, keep various secrets. So, to keep these secrets, these government organizations have to make sure that the data are protected so they use cryptosystems to protect important information.

Cryptography has been a huge factor in military victories and failures. It is used to spot treason. It is also used for espionage and business advantage. It is used for both warfare and economic espionage.

Cryptography is also used by security agencies most specifically the National Security Agency. The government employs many cryptographers to help decode the intelligence messages sent throughout the world. Cryptology is also used to determine the plans of terrorists and other threats to national and global security.

Recently, Edward Snowden revealed that the NSA has numerous surveillance programs. They monitor calls and even emails. But, how does the NSA hack emails? Well, by using clock arithmetic (modular arithmetic) and elliptic curve cryptography. NSA checks private emails by reverse-engineering a way to forecast the outcome of elliptic curve cryptography. This is how the NSA hacks into the emails of certain individuals.

3. Banks

Banks and other financial institutions use cryptography to protect their clients from forgery and other types of fraud. They also use cryptosystems to authenticate the identities of their clients.

ATMs also use cryptography. In fact, most ATMs operate using system that uses a secret key called "PIN key". This PIN is derived using the Data Encryption Standard or DES. In the early development stages of ATMs, banks usually use IBM encryption products to encrypt the PIN. But, nowadays, banks use a device called a "security module". This module is placed in a safe and it contains all the PINs and the keys in the bank. Only the mainstream programmers of that bank can see the PIN. This is the reason banks that are part of the Mastercard and Visa networks use these security modules.

4. Businesses

Aside from banks and financial institutions, businesses can also benefit from cryptosystems. It is no secret that corporate espionage is common nowadays. A lot of corporations hire professional spies to steal information from their competitors. So, to prevent this from happening, you have to protect your government organizations.

5. Terrorists and Rebel Groups

Cryptography is powerful and neutral. It can both benefit and destroy communities and people. A lot of rebel groups intercept a large variety of data transported through secured networks from instant messaging, satellite collision prevention, to flight tower communication management. Remember that when you're inputting your Facebook log-in information or making a credit card payment over the internet, you're using a certain fundamental encryption that, in other countries, could be used by rebels and terrorists to organize a protest or an attack.

In fact, in 2015, the terrorists who attacked Paris used encrypted apps to hide their plot. The results of the investigation show that the terrorists used Telegram and WhatsApp. Both of these applications have an end-to-end encryption that's difficult to decrypt. This encryption was designed to protect the privacy of the users. These apps were used by the terrorists to communicate moments before the attacks.

Aside from using heavily encrypted apps, the people responsible for the 2015 Paris attacks use several other methods to cover their tracts, including using pre-paid cellphone sim cards to prevent surveillance.

Cryptography is everywhere. It is used to secure your email, your social media accounts, your bank account, and even your gaming accounts. Cryptography is no longer just that fancy security measure that military people use to communicate plots and defense schemes.

Cryptography Laws

There are a number of laws that governs cryptography all over the globe. This is to ensure that messages are transported securely and confidentially. It is designed to keep the encryption schemes out of the hands of unauthorized people and foreign powers. Various governments have implemented different tools to transform the data via encryption technology and to prevent unauthorized access to these data. There are four basic cryptography laws – patent issues, import control, and export control.

- Patent Issues

Most cipher algorithms are patented. So, there are laws that protect the intellectual property of different forms of ciphers and encryption such as technologies that are used for:

- Keeping email exchanges private
- Securing internet financial transactions
- Authenticating websites

The intellectual property laws governing encryption usually go hand in hand with the import laws.

- Import Control Laws

This law restricts the use of some types of cryptography in specific countries. So, there are local laws and international agreements that prohibit the importation of specific types of cryptographic technologies. Some governments prohibit the import of the cryptographic technologies to protect local businesses and prevent unfair competition. Import of encryption protocols that threaten legitimate businesses.

- Export Control Laws

There are a number of export control laws that govern cryptographic technologies that have a huge impact on matters of national security. For example, businesses are not allowed to export encryption and decryption technologies that are used by the NSA.

- Search and Seizure

There are some laws that compel a person to reveal an encryption key or decrypt data files. For example, suspected terrorists are compelled to decrypt a file that contains strategies and plans of attack. These laws are highly contested because it is in conflict with one's right against self-incrimination.

If you're in the cryptology business, it is necessary to know the basic law governing encryption protocols and devices.

Conclusion

Thank you again for downloading this book!

I hope this book was able to help you master the basics of cryptography.

The next step is to build your personal cryptosystems so you can easily encrypt messages.

Finally, if you enjoyed this book, please take the time to share your thoughts and post a review on Amazon. It'd be greatly appreciated!

Thank you and good luck!